An English Nazareth

D1599967

Presented to Purchase College
by
Gary Waller, PhD Cambridge

State University of New York
Distinguished Professor

Professor
of Literature & Cultural
Studies, and Theatre &
Performance, 1995-2019
Provost 1995-2004

Martyn Crucefix

An English
Nazareth

ENITHARMON PRESS

First published in 2004
by the Enitharmon Press
26B Caversham Road
London NW5 2DU

www.enitharmon.co.uk

Distributed in the UK by
Central Books
99 Wallis Road
London E9 5LN

Distributed in the USA and Canada
by Dufour Editions Inc.
PO Box 7, Chester Springs
PA 19425, USA

© Martyn Crucefix 2004

ISBN 1 900564 14 9

British Library Cataloguing-in-Publication Data.
A catalogue record for this book is available
from the British Library.

Typeset in Bembo by Servis Filmsetting Ltd
and printed in England by
Antony Rowe Ltd

ACKNOWLEDGEMENTS

Some of these poems, or earlier versions of them, appeared in the following places: *Acumen, The Bound Spiral, The Interpreter's House, Leviathan, The Poem* (www.thepoem.co.uk), *Magma, Poetry London, Poetry Street N16, Poetry Wales, Stand, The Reader, The Tabla Book of New Verse, Thumbscrew.*

An earlier version of 'So far' was first published in *The New Exeter Book of Riddles*, eds. Kevin Crossley-Holland and Lawrence Sail (Enitharmon, 1999); 'The brief occasion of Bosko and Admira' was a prize winner in the Stand International Poetry Competition, 1998; 'Crumple zone' won first prize in the Middlesex Full Circle Arts Project Poetry Competition 1999; 'On night's estate' was a prize winner in the London Writers' Competition 2001; 'The gate' won second prize in the Leicester Open Poetry Competition 2003; 'An English Nazareth' and 'A boy's errand' received awards in the Ware Poets Open Poetry Competition 2003.

My thanks to Andrew Brenner, Neil Curry, Mario Petrucci, Myra Schneider, Sarah Van Gogh and Brett Van Toen for their invaluable comments.

This book is dedicated to my parents.

CONTENTS

I

II

III

I

A boy's errand

I go to Spar and Mr Adams
who drops his small hands
beneath the counter
where it's already wrapped
in white tissue paper.
Crisp, soft and undisturbed,
I carry it close to my chest,
the length of my forearm,
palm flat to one end.
It's like something asleep.
It seems crisper today –
the pressure of my fingers
telling the birth-smell
of heat, yeast, risen air.
The confining tin
held sides to softness
and the crusty burst,
split down the length,
sharp-edged and breakable,
caramelly across my tongue.
And each bite a glimpse –
one leading to the next
till I'm nuzzling in,
jaggedness on my cheeks
being bitten, biting deep
through crust to white flesh
as if there were a heart
unconsumed somewhere
I might lay my hands on
bring back to the house.

The gate

Was inch-tubular for economy's sake,
a post-war issue for a self-built house.
Hammerite black now, but once white,

earlier cream, its soft curves and corners
a rough square hung between cement posts.
A big-thumbed latch on the left –

beside it, a schematic sun-rise of tubing –
beneath, the squared-off wire grid
I'd work my toes in for the springy dip

of my weight on the straining hinges.
I'd hook elbows in and swing and swing.
A jarring crash and decrescendo –

the muddy-booted, casual back-heel
of my brother after football on the grass.
The gentle clink-clank of the sneck as Mum

bent to secure it with as much care as she
shook slippy fried eggs onto my plate.
The half-way firm, suddenly stunned

impact as Dad's hand swiped, held shut:
his sluggish pirouette before the flowers,
home from work with an empty Thermos.

And me, arms shaking at the tiny ridges
of concrete under my trike, Dad stooping
to frame the cream gate, the hedge beyond,

the telegraph wires converging on clouds,
wires dividing bright weather with the effort
to remember – until now it appears

all that muddle of love has so long gone
unremarked between us there is no need
to listen for it, though a bad day shows

every possible latch broken – yet another
effortlessly finds the point of purchase,
the give and spring and swerve and space.

17 Britannia Square

To keep it steady, I stand on the bottom rung.
The galvanised ladder from a neighbour's shed
creaks and squeals under your stepping weight.
It sounds like coins being scraped together.
Last to leave, I could not manage ten minutes
in charge of your tall, Edwardian house.
Since I forgot to bring the key – rung on rung,
self-conscious as no real intruder would be,
now you find a way through your own walls.
And if we did not then, we might once have done
this kind of thing – the cat-burgling high-jinks,
a pair of students climbing to college windows
against vigilant authority, as then, after a drink,
loose-tongued and having – as Keats once called it –
not a dispute, but a disquisition on how a man
could possess no determined self, like a state
that sees no need of a constitution.
Now that looks as much risk as opportunity.
I see you pull up the sash, begin to wriggle
into your bathroom and it seems less a truth
to last beyond our teens. Your hips, your knees
and disappearing calves, your feet – swallowed,
but for a tiny back kick, one heel cracking
a window pane, white star-burst like a rifle shot,
as you vanish at last, absorbed to your house,
your job, your family. All the while I wait below
in love with mine. In the minutes it takes you
to come downstairs, laughing, unlock the door,
I see you drop from the black, splintered pane,
sprawl, bruised and quivering as a newly-born
in your college room – then up and alert,
the strangeness of our futures a thing yet to learn.

Wish it was the Sixties

You are thinking of your father
waxing cotton wool before a swim,

his almost naked, bulky presence
as the waves thrash in

cold and English and full of salt
and frighteningly a part

of the oceans you hear about,
their whelming storms, slick monsters,

drowning pools, knot-tugging wrack
which must never be far off

even ten feet from the sand's edge,
at one with the mix of the seaside

the horror and the tedium.
You loved him so much then

while his shorts flapped on his thighs,
the cotton wool rolled tight,

pushed into his ears, something to do
with balance. It kept him safe.

So far

A whole world involved in me. Open up and gaze.
Like God, I give rise to novelties like *parbuckle,*
the bright *pardelote,* or pain-killing *paregoric.*
It smacks of Paradise as you enviously seek
through my broken gate, realise the perfect myth
of first to last things has already been achieved.
It's what art and science only dream of doing.
But think of me as crutch, as friend, as fall-back
for your ignorance only so far. Beware.
Hard as you might look, you are not mentioned here.

An English Nazareth

(In 1061, Lady Richeldis of Walsingham, in a series of visions,
received instructions to build a replica of Christ's home)

We – who have only our strength to sell
and so little here to be thankful for –
we know well she has never risen
from that embroidered footstool
where she embroiders her mornings.
Yet she has stood in His simple home,
she says, the woodshavings obvious
on the clay floor, the cramp, the cool.
And because she has power over us
to manufacture walls out of English
ground, to her specifications
(though she insists, not hers at all;
she's only a witness to the original),
because of this her dream has weight.
Here, a slant of evening sun, the saw
still warm in the red-grained wood.
Here, the hammer's shout on the nail
each time bursting and then dying off
as she passes a door out of Palestine.
In an ecstasy, at least three times –
though not moving one tailor's inch
off that embroidered footstool
where we imagine her long fingers
fumbling over the detail in her lap –
we picture her there, tall and swaying
richly through Christ's small house.
And no matter how vivid her dream,
local men build as we have always built:
English wood upon English earth.
The best we deliver is a mockery,

a cacked version of our own poor homes
(those shambles she's never visited)
yet this is the one she will have us deck
with flowers, have us light, keep warm,
proof from rain, since this is the roof
under which she expects to dwell
long in grace, in that other real place.
While we – who have only ourselves to sell –
give praise to God for the gift of work.

The author of *Kosmos*

(Alexander von Humboldt)

He is a good-looking man,
though his particular vanity lies
in the pursuit of flowers,
of which he takes good care,
purchases fine linen for his shoulders,
a rich waistcoat, loose neckerchief.

The long stripe of his breeches
bulges with the braced thigh
as he turns to view us,
tousled, frankly endearing,
before the book
he has broken off from ruling.

More than competence
breathing beneath dark palms.
He is far from Europe,
so much the discoverer of species
as to think of himself
as an inventor.

The sprigs he holds are his darlings,
laid out on sheets,
blooms that resemble heads,
reclined, disorganised leaves,
eager to be ushered under his hand
to the index of knowledge
before their lank-haired sisters,
who rise around, darkly serrated,
locks of rope-thick midnight,
stepping a descent
he has already climbed.

And further off, subsequent lands
ride in the ocean, provocative,
buoyant, populous, fragmentary,
breaking off clues to their existence,
casting them into the flood.

Eating out

So little evidence left
of hours in which the sun set
and turned up the volume
on the sienna of the hillside,
as we sat in the garden
and saw unleashed,
the deeper blues of sky
and strewn the white of stars
that rose to us irreversibly,
while we too lit candles
and settled about the tabletop.
We ate, drank and watched,
in the absence of gods,
benign, as the world shrugged
and sank away on all sides,
pared to the flick of a bat's
black glove in the eaves.
Then the whole earth
shrunk to the table and we,
some immured museum,
marble seance, our great feet
sunk in darkness and grass,
accorded the simplicity
of head and torso alone,
our poorly lit busts beside
human remains of a meal:
a circuit of illumination
that later unwound,
paraded to the back door,
a triumph of unsteady light,
of iron and plate and glass,
the little shadows we know.

Dolmen at Skyber Hen

One of the last molars of the county
peers through misted windows to where
we spend a candlelit Christmas Day

in a converted barn we treat as home,
eating Turkish Delight, liqueur trifles,
kiwi and kumquat and dates,

the cream and purple of ham on the bone,
high octane chocolate, nuts
and berries so far beyond the staple.

Its shadowy, toothy crenellations
bring back days of hunt and kill, pulling
down blood in this brief daylight,

yet we celebrate the new religion –
grown old in just two thousand years,
so my own children hesitate to name

the mother and father of Jesus Christ.
They cannot say why a weakling child
was born in straw like a sacrifice.

The giving of gifts is a simpler delight.
And the excess of everything makes
more sense under the dolmen's weight,

unmoved beneath stars we see tonight
without the blind of civilisation.
So one comes in breathless with cold,

with starlight in her lungs as if to say
prodigality gives rise to its own
gestures: a reply to ice-plates, stiffened

slush and mud's miracle of iron crust,
the wind's sheaf of sharpened knives –
every bitter provocation to give more

and more than we can reasonably afford –
useless in the end, though it will resound
long after these older, equivocal gifts.

Organised rain

The phrase you come with,
   laughing up the stairwell
from the late-night forecast
   and into the bedroom,
sets us giggling so much
   we stir our boy from sleep
like a storm off the south coast
   disorganised, turning.

His cry sets me back
   to thunder-broken afternoons –
he could barely sit alone
   and I'd prop him on the sill
to watch the garden trees,
   their slow-motion splintering,
every stretch and flounce
   unfolding in the breeze.

And though my head
   was at his very shoulder,
I could not see what he did,
   what set his throat roaring,
arms milling in the wind
   as storm clouds came on:
to be gone like fortune's child
   from books we now read him.

Then imagine, years on,
   his returning to our door –
now a wide-eyed, grown man,
   finally stopped to listen
to *pit-pat* becoming downpour
   over the smoking rooftops,
that sweet irresolution
   he comes asking us to name.

The blackwater doctor

(The scales of the tench exude a slime
thought to have healing properties)

The hidden outlet spelt us food,
its unpredictable disgorging
of coloured water from bank to bank,
a creamy spate of frothing milk,
a watery Crosse & Blackwell brew,
the skimmings, the dregs, the washings
of industrial gruel, flushed out
to bring the best specimens,
so we hoped, to hooks and lines.

It might even have been true,
since that summer we heard nothing
of other acrid stuff
quietly seeping down the river chains.
Happily, we knotted rod-bags
to cross-bars, crept in the after-dawn
through mists standing to nettle height,
stalking the twitch of green lilies,
signs of the blackwater doctor
and the slab-sides of carp.
We bent to flick red and yellow
and orange tips of day-glo floats
into the mouth of the tunnel.

Come November, the river had risen,
closing in on armpits and eyes.
Water blanked itself more completely
in upstream muds, though still
it roiled and tugged and disappointed us.
We pedalled home with only
an eddying remnant of its power,

though still night after night I'd stand
deep in that tunnel mouth,
staring down the long lens at hooks
and leads and live-bait and line
spattering round me, thickening a broth,
rich and opaque and on its way.

Reading *The Quiet American* again

Becomes more and more of a mystery
why the smart-aleck of an idealist chose
this book for the Henson Memorial Prize
on the square, green-clothed table,
dead centre the wooden stage,
its bright orange Penguin spine winking
among the black mortars and gowns
of the last years of the county grammar schools.

Nothing here resembles what he knew –
the back-streets and sky-drowned fields
of old Vietnam, the gravel-drawl of Fowler,
that quintessential cut of Greene,
who gave the book its most remembered moment:
he wakes to find his hand
where it had always lain at night between her legs.

Stuff that stirred a sixteen-year-old's blood,
though an image of uxorious habit,
not the moistened thrills we handed dog-eared round.
And the guy loses the girl to the priggish,
juice-drinking, innocent American
with his long books, important father, earnestness
and efficiency – so in love with torch-lifting
Liberty that, later, it was his obedient boys
who fell on the quiet of My Lai.

Nothing could be more remote from him
than the angry, wived and loveless Fowler –
the dithering male, well-meaning despite himself,
with his envy of the godded, faithlessness
in himself, his trying to decipher
the arrogance and politeness of the quiet American
he thought too dangerous to live . . .

But embarrassed, and proud of it too,
shaking hands with the cloaked headmaster
for a paperback I must have chosen
by title alone, must have thought apt
and likely to please the quick, quiet schoolboy
who that night in bed broke the spine
and was appalled to read innocence already dead,
the book's sole intent to show it had to happen.

The Philosopher's Garden

You push four-month-old Jacob and we talk,
though my mind is full of *The Winter's Tale*.

More ugly sculpture from a local artist
has appeared in The Philosopher's Garden

and the Priory Café Bernie ran for years
has a new frontage, new paint, a new name.

We patronise it anyway. Sit and choose
decent coffee and panini, no longer find

the old stale doughnut and metallic tea.
A rocky shoreline. A poor coincidence.

Shakespeare wrote the kind of ship he loved
and broke it on the coast of Bohemia.

A clown to witness men drown at sea;
a shepherd to recover the swaddled girl.

Together, the pair of them, thick-witted
and visionary, meeting with things dying

and with things new-born . . .
As we leave you talk of your father, how he

was dignified and tall, a talker like you,
his words and phrases on your tongue now

taste of his kiss and the back of his hand.
The buggy starts to drift. You begin to cry

for the world as it is, a place like this,
where a man so sharp and patient as he

has to die slowly, his body past control
and to say, as we do, he grew a child again

is to disguise a terrible thing . . .
We walk in The Philosopher's Garden.

The buggy I push rattles empty now.
Arms full, in your mind *The Winter's Tale*.

The umbrella and the bay tree

(i.m. Laurence Bowkett)

By seven-thirty, you are with us all
tonight in the gloom of *The Washington*,
though we omit you from every round.
Powerless as the laral gods who gave you
no protection, even *laurus nobilis,*

the bay tree I bought you, proved no use.
Today, I searched 570 and 790,
in the Dewey decimal classification
your fingers ran through a thousand times,
for the facts of death and prolific life:

as if I looked for you now and you then.
You taught shard-life and careful fieldwork,
the near-dead language of not giving in.
You offered the heroic a modern face,
though death proved the more determined.

You understood lives alter what they touch:
a house, a street, a flowering tree,
for those who know us are not struck dumb,
a library unread the moment we die.
They roar like a lantern with our life inside.

In Hornsey Central at 570
this morning, I found books to undermine
my daughter's smiling confidence
that bugs she crushes beneath her shoe
lie dead a while, then revive good as new.

At 790 I leafed through life and death
in Ancient Egypt for her older brother:
how they wash their dead in water and oil,

then bind them in linen smeared with gum
and priests wrap lucky charms inside

in hope that none will break the seal
till the dead themselves in time of need.
So for you I'll wrap Homer, Wolves black-
and-gold, your Micra, Marvel, Blockley
and booze, moist, sweet cake for the road,

Frederick Leighton, Sir Frankie Howerd,
Wisden, The Smiths and that Italian umbrella
you flourished one day and thundered open –
behold! the Sistine roof appeared
to keep your bald head from the hissing rain.

II

All Hallows

All night I work my front door
    for ghouls and witches,
open it to a rainy darkness
    hanging back-drop for them –
cocky, come demanding
    to my face, curt simple threats
to the level of my waist.

I am ready to meet them,
    with crisps and chocolate,
sweets, biscuits, chocolate again
    for these are sweet-toothed
dwarves, clips of dreams,
    whose black ill-cut capes
soon return to the night

having done us no harm.
    Rather they draw us out,
our stepped-up go-betweens,
    their talent to turn back
from the dazzle of indoors.
    But come morning,
shapes of children are lying

shrunken on my doorstep:
    grotesque, pot-bellied, beaming
glycerine and sugar dolls,
    let slip like orphans
I cannot attend to now.
    I step round them, dissolving
in the mouth of the rain.

Casserole and closed mussels

Think of popcorn. A shatter of shells
   multiplying inside. The lid
punched instantly into mid-air.

Every mussel a pause, a comma.
   A pan full of hesitation
to take off the top of your head.

Now imagine touching them.
   All edge. And severity.
You are repelled. This is black art.

The Cleverly boy

Grace had gone early,
  tired after mowing both lawns.
I'd washed cups and saucers.
  Plugs and lights out.

Quiet on the stairs.
  Sounds of a heavy roller,
stones popping the pavement,
  I pulled back the curtain.

Over the lawn, beyond the hedge,
  the Cleverly boy and another
lugging and pushing like crazy –
  a cement mixer,

its gaping squat barrel
  pointing directly at me.
I sat across from them in court.
  The police were delighted.

But they got bail and pending.
  Grace wanted to sleep in.
First snow had been forecast,
  so it was cold as I crept

to the landing, drew the curtain.
  On the fresh white of the lawn,
scraped down to the green
  FUCKING GRASS

Clay Town

This is a one trade town
and ours is the glaze
makes men and women,
whores and dealers rise
to display their wares
before the middle classes.
The butcher, the baker,
the two blind brothers
who run the corner store
agree. Clay Town,
from far east to west,
knows one thing well:
the price of terracotta,
of twenty thousand lips
and their dusty interiors.
The dripped-glaze rims
and the punctured sides
of purse-mouthed jars
that want bright flowers.
The wide-mouthed roars,
the cracked and distressed,
the spun and the coil
with memories of grain,
of first-press virgin oil
so clear and profound
it might once have thought.
Unsweetened dreams
are the wrong sort
as titanic bellies yawn,
gawp of the steakhouse,
ash welcomes the urn
and nothing will save us.

The green-handled knife

Happens every bloody time.
The hygiene boys' harangue slips my mind

as I start with brimming white silk in vats.
Enough to douse twenty Cleopatras,

I imagine them – a ruck of arms, milky-wet,
and drip-laced breasts licked by it.

I jerk the giant stirrers on.
They begin their slow-motion spin

and it's back to blue metal vats
and eyes at 'view-points' built to hold them back.

The culture in. I let the whole lot stew.
Always there's plenty else to do:

yesterday's batches waiting to be wrapped,
compressed into tins, packed.

Eyes come and go every five minutes.
Now pour in the rennet.

The bath grows grainy, blows a thick sleet.
I turn and stir it.

When it's a blizzard
of curd

and it's time to drain off the whey,
they turn to the little ones: *Miss Muffet*, they say.

It's me, you fucks!
I'm the angel in white wellies and white kecks,

white hat, whey-faced. Look!
Now your entry makes up half my week

why not watch me and fall in love with work,
with my shovelling out the musty curd

and then compare it to what you do.
I thank you.

The boredom in your eye wilts at the sight
of my green-handled knife.

I slit
the curd's throat

to breezeblock shapes, so clean –
cut igloo pieces of trembling cream,

add salt in a shower of gritty rain,
fling it through the crumblers and into a tin

and tomorrow you will have moved on
to the rope-maker, the bloody rare-breeds farm.

Metaphysics and Mr Marvel

It's what Paracelsus and Cornelius Agrippa
risked their eyes and cracked eye-teeth for:

slip coppers in boxes and open them gold.
He blows up balloons and you watch as they

bulge at the wrong end and it's not pretend!
His gallon of water's a genuine mystery:

he douses a child, but the child stays dry!
He does it with a rap and an *alla-ka-zam*

and all performed in a star-spangled cloak.
He arrives – a spectacle – on his own bike,

but pulling a trailer he padlocks to the gate.
He does life from nothing – fur balls in a hat!

Action at a distance – the egg's in your ear!
The mind-body problem – a hypnotist's trick!

Astonishing, isn't it? You know he will make
you vanish in a flash, come back in smoke:

cause and effect ripped to shreds in his shears.
He breaks every curb on the will-be and is.

And to top the lot, Mr Marvel can appear,
simultaneously, both here and there –

though that's less magic and more the power
of a strong franchise – for Mr Marvel

has so many forms from great to less-good
to wish-to-hell-you-never-booked-him.

Though don't push that to any conclusion.
If it was really more than your average toy,

some matter of fact you were searching for,
would your finger be so keen to punch his dial?

Would you come in search of distraction?
I'm sorry? No – his is the only name on file.

You know Alan Mills

He's on Centre Court as soon as rain falls.
        A judicious look
and a buttoned suit, shoving his hair back.
        His kids must love him
for what he does. Like TV presenting,
        it looks so effortless
that kind of job – and it probably is.
        It's what we'd all like
and thought we'd get just a few years back.
        The power of the man –
on his yea or nay crowds cheer or groan.
        But here is my point:
in the interim, does Alan just wait
        in the dressing-room,
feel his importance like a comfortable home?
        It's like Maryann,
when we talk careers. Yes, she wants one,
        but her ambition
'since I was about five' is television –
        it's just to be there,
preternaturally bright in a million ears,
        maybe dancing for sure
to cross legs and smile, introduce and turn –
        above all, for this:
to ensure down-time, freedom to relax.
        Just the kind of life
I read about back in the old Renault Five
        (the white not the brown)
my girlfriend drove around '79.
        Perhaps our best time,
the Yorkshire Peaks, after my Finals exam,
        I read industrial/
social revolution, climbed a hill,

as my working life
was about to begin and those on the Left
became distraught
at the changing face of the shape of work.
Not enough to go round.
The powerful, the rich would close their hand
and the working poor
in their millions would work no more.
New Statesman and *Sun*
were worried in 1979,
but Alan – even then –
scanned London sky and was looking slim.
Now I tell Maryann
to give it up, her talk of television –
since her usual report
greater effort required is the bitch we live with
and then we die.

The dream of the broken exhaust

My chained hand sleeps
    suddenly on the wing mirror.
An unerring eye for halter-backs,
    long legs in lemon,
fragments of football, little kits
    swinging in the rear-view mirror.

In sight of – is it? – Bedfordshire,
    after miles of woof
and fart and blurting exhaust.
    These territories with it:
in love with look-alike GTIs,
    their built-up cellulite arches

and almost cherish plates,
    the blue and white signs
flagging temptation,
    due north or due south,
since all directions
    leave this floodlit drive-thru

where boys sit in one-eyed cars,
    windows rolled to the rubber,
elbows crooked
    and eyeing the skidmarks,
the glittering hopeless hulls
    of a jammed Bank Holiday –

each roped to another,
    the orange vertebrae of light
down the curved and roaring
    oil-spilt back of England
that cannot be young again,
    does not know how to grow up.

Scoop

Now that our values are 'real',
I mean weighed by the ounce,
all my money shrinks,
pockets full of pieces.
Like the ancient Greeks,
whose coins grew small,
they are kept in the mouth
like a wad of tobacco,
but worth not as much.
It's hardly encouraging
to make a man save.
They taste like blood.
Can't do me any good.
Even give me ideas
I'd rather not own.
Home late, long dark,
my eldest daughter, me.
I josh her along.
You want a few pence?
She shifts in the dark.
We get real close.
The scoop of her tongue
takes them from my mouth.

On Bunhill Fields

Strange fruit for a central London tree.
    For a moment old girlfriends crowd me:
legs spread and balanced on a branch for me,
    the shocking sight of pink play-mate Barbie.
Ah, now I see what is really going on:
    child drops it and wails all the way home.
Samaritan intent on righting wrong.
    She's been out all night and that's too long.

Bedraggled and party-torn and partly-torn,
    afro-blonde hair the colour of real corn,
spattered, shoeless and better off not born.
    All the girls I've known, I left them for dead.
It's OK, I guess. I imagine them in bed.
    Looking like Barbie. Can't think what I said.

Try looking up

It loops over the parapet,
red/white markings, beginnings
of harmonic wobble in the tail
growing to circular motion
as it stirs the air behind it,
falling unintendedly accurate,
whack across the windscreen,
a giant fluid-bursting bug,
a dribble of brown,
the remains a white shell
into the slipstream
and I've not seen the road,
the sky, the verge, even
followed the slack hand
that lobbed it and forgot,
though for a moment, there,
the arm's little muscles
strung from shoulder to neck,
not even thinking his crap
can drop and if it kills
there's no reason to pause,
since half a mile further on
it's the car-driver gets it,
the thigh-drilling adrenalin
that thumps and veers him
onto the hard shoulder,
where he sits and stares
at the carriageway roar,
a coke container afloat,
light and capped, straw intact,
looping over the parapet.

The girl who didn't dance

A sixth-form party on a Friday night.
The badminton court of the village hall
regained its white angles as the dance floor cleared.
When our story dropped from the papers at last,
I realised how much I'd fancied Liz,
with her freckled face, hair combed to shining slats,
long and straight to her beginning breasts.
How much her friend terrified me:
Patsy, with her big hips, chest and baritone voice,
though once I'd seen scratched on her desk
the hand writes and having writ moves on.

I wanted to read it again on Monday,
when Bill was in plaster up to his thighs,
Paul stitched across his purple forehead.
The girl I'd been with, though we didn't dance,
came to me early on the Saturday morning,
her eyes red and angry, her hair untidy
as if filled with unspent electricity.
I knew how much comforting she'd need
as she stood and sobbed at the news.

I thought of nothing but the childish game
we'd played in the back of her father's car,
both ducking out of sight
as the headlights swung the bend
to catch the four of them, thumbs-up for a lift –
the boys ahead, then behind, a bright fan,
the shoulder-spread of Liz's blonde hair.
And beyond, Patsy's rolling swagger,
her great white face turned back to the light,
exactly as the drunk will have seen them,
five minutes later, on the heel of the bridge,
as he drove into their white arms like skittles.

Crumple zone

It's as if a car
were a cake of semtex,
a bundle of gelignite candles
to break open the bank,
the time-lock,
where it slews across
the central reservation,
bounding like a colt,
the wildness of youth
shaken out like hair
in a collapse of steel,
of crumple zones,
her hands, pale jokes
slithering on the wheel,
till out of nothing,
that terrific shaking
father would always give
before his big hands
did what they liked
and sailed right out
of her understanding
and under her clothes,
sharpening his breath
with horrid concentration,
sinking on her shoulder,
as if twenty years
had never happened,
as if she'd not gunned away,
eyes fixed to the road
and kept going, going.

Sculpting sand

I walk in the tide-marked jumble
of bladders, wood, weed, plastics –
the little pools where I fished up
urchin lives, only now to release them,

remembering the beginning of it
in the fact of the tides
and how my father would help me
to slope-walled castles, a moat, a gatehouse

that withstood all I could imagine
and then crumpled in minutes
once the waves slid to them.
How I learnt to call it by name.

How I drew more extravagant shapes
to its desolating edge – a two-fingered
fuck you, part gift, part sacrifice,
partly therapeutic.

Dragons haul themselves from the dunes,
wedge-jawed with the effort,
muscled front legs drawing
grains together beneath the surface –

and all implied by my hand.
A triumph of horse, hoofed and real,
about to dissolve into the foam-maned waves.
A club-wielding, yellow Triton

I'd have dipping his toe into defeat.
A Nativity. A telephone.
A TV screen sinking back
into the salt and pepper shifting morass.

All these works and days by water
conclude at the edge of an ocean
that grows more envious to come on board.
I stoop to pick a set of dentures,

grinning like a crystalline wedge,
a sea-worked set of ivory organ pipes,
the inner fluting of a great bone
moiled by the sea and sand and wind:

whatever it might once have been,
something has been left for me
in the tangled stir-fry of the sea's edge,
a little comedy at last.

III

Tortoise

Drop-jawed and pink-tongued
  with what appears pleasure,
though it's unlikely. Long drawn
  love of a shell's chill desire.
Scaly touch. His gasping breath
  and her earthbound silence.

What if every tide was drawn
  drily barking one to another?
Claws, tendrils in cold oceans
  get a purchase on pleasures
lying buried in prehistory.
  What if two stones can be tender?

Tiger

I had a tiger suck my fist last night.
A warm, wet clasp that owed everything

to the child who yesterday held my thumb.
Sleep changed her to this striped killer

though I felt no fear, nor could I see
why the world was not as I'd been told.

Its canines were yellowed, big as my thumb.
My hand glistened, saliva-wrinkled.

I saw the cat plead just as it was shot –
its crew-cut pelt punctured five times

each blast received like an electric shock,
growing less and less . . .

Spreadeagled across the bonnet of a jeep
at the mud village, a thousand file past

to touch a paw, stroke a hollowed ear.
The cat, last night, hung so leaden-heavy

on my hand as did the child yesterday,
a warm, wet mouth wanting everything.

The cross on the Chevin

1. For the man who played Jesus

She has cried all morning,
type-cast herself in the role,
long-drawn wail for Good Friday.
All the more haunting
as there's no apparent cause,
for she is fed, dry, wrapped warm,
at thirteen months, unfamiliar
with either the lie or the truth.

In church we cannot stifle her noise
for the drama of Easter,
so she's walked on the streets
through a tumbling rain,
grievously, as we two argue
who ought to have taken her,
who would have liked to remain,
where, for how long,
quarrelling over divisions of labour.
Our little girl is passionate
and innocent as the sodden air,
as you act out Christ's stagger,
trick the congregation
up the scale of tears.

2. The cross on the Chevin

On a hill above the wet town,
rising forty feet from sunken concrete girders
and held to vertical
by hawsers of plaited steel,
I hear singing in the wind.
Needle-thin voices – in my experience,
the kind of clarity and precision
expressed only by unalloyed matter.

This, the greatest of machines.
A geometrical presence,
it gives the impression of being built
to douse its surroundings,
drown them in a blacked-out tarn.
Its brutal juncture offers no help
in what we know will come.

3. Ascension Day

I have watched these three years
and, to the day, they come back,
intent on the air above our roofs,
above our heads, where we loaf
tonight with no more to do
than kick over the crack-up
of our adjoining paths,
neighbourly plans at the margin.

And into our fine silence
they come flying. The whisper
of returning swallows beats up
under the eaves of a house
you laugh has been leaning
further and further
with every year you remain.

Belief will not fail us tonight –
our children separately stowed,
shut-eyed sons and daughters.
We are their shambolic crew,
turning out on deck to watch
the dwindling of light,
the shift and swell beneath us,
the homecoming of birds
staking out their soft periodic.

A brace of saints

(from a painting by F. N. Souza)

Two of them in the desert – unlikely
as quenching bottles, both ready to spurt.
One has chosen to appear in a blue shirt.
Contrasting red preferred by the other.

The saintly set little store by teamwork.
This one, for example, is bearded and bald.
The second has breasts and careful hair.
This one, though far from home, has hold

of a black twig like a bird's severed claw.
The saintly find cause, then set to work:
such things as the scab of urban sprawl,
its own restlessness that of a spread-

eagled patient left in a corridor,
though the city boasts its tall blue buildings
and towers no longer trumpeting smoke.
So a brace of saints cross desert places.

In their billowing wake, they leave behind
spiritual footprints filling up with sand.
They see that belief has no rival here
and the saintly soon make easy choices

once they realise everything is for sale.
The blue-grey smog of the material
pricks and chases – white letters on a wall
protest: LISTEN TO THE PEOPLE.

Aerial display

Featureless today, a great blue
barely scuffed by cloud,
remote shreds and pimplings
at the hill-edged horizon.
Banks of woolly cumulus
are what we had hoped for,
but the stiff-ribbed benches,
seem painful by calculation,
keep us craned at the sky
for movement in the air
which is invisible, we know,
even to those who inhabit it.
We anticipate a black speck,
trained, precise and rowing
wings in search of thermals
that today come lumbering
from hedge intersection
to copse fence junction,
a clutter of wedged roofs.
We each salute the sun,
grown grainy and provisional.
Then the shout goes up
and she is already at stoop,
touching a hundred miles an hour.
Our eyes chase her folded clod,
a swooning shovel-full
of control through thin air,
too fast for the change
in our dropping focus,
the sky razed beyond her
as she cuts us all to ribbons.
Then she's at his glove,
panting on a metre of leash,
assured, replete, demure.

The natural history of Stanhoe

I drive through more carnage
than in the last Act of *King Lear*,
lifeless and twisted, the gaping
of split fur and feather
ridden into the sodden roadside.

More even than I remember
in Oxford covered market,
near Christmas-time.
Bloody-nosed hare, rabbit, pheasant,
so far advanced in their fall
to the table
it was impossible to imagine them
alive to sight and scent.

Soon as I arrive, I take down
the kitchen's suburban nets,
wanting the best view of fields
I rented this houseful of windows for
and a fledgeling, softly,
impacts on the glass.

I ease the dusty window.
I lean from the paint-blistered edge,
squinnying to see the tiny smash:
a cripple-winged bird
I can do nothing with
but go and kneel down beside it,
spread my palms to the gravel
where it dies and then to the daylight
I stripped of obstruction,
now clear as sweet water
through the heart of the house.

This is all of it

Stepping through two doors of the aviary,
he blurs behind close mesh.
I look up at him, standing like a big tree,
the birds, tail-heavy
in the halo of their own wing-blur,
settle on arms,
shoulders, his grinning head.
They must tickle like snowflakes.

For years he drove freight trains.
I saw him one afternoon at Westbury Station,
leaning from the tiny
high cab window,
peaked cap on his baldness,
one hand visible,
pointing to the engine around him
as if to say
this is it, this is all of it.

Or did I dream that.
Hardly matters, now I learn at third-hand
he's fallen from his bed,
suddenly finished,
knowing he will have expected
the kind of heaven I don't believe in –
though as distance
lays itself down between Bob and me,
I grow less sure of the great divide,
what I saw
from what I might have seen.

Say, I stood and watched him go,
step on blurring step
through the door, hands quiet at his sides,
ready and waiting
for what I sometimes hear,
a whir of anxiousless wings,
perfectly clear.

Tracy Island

(from Thunderbird 5)

It's not all palm trees as people expect.
When we were small, I'd climb to a high cleft,
my arms braced against trunk and branch
to make a wedged parallelogram
from which I could look down on it all,
my brothers beetling below. I'd grow
dizzy, euphoric with the sense of control,
the great green beast . . .

I'd hear father first, calling us to listen.
He could unlock the confusion of things:
Think of the unfortunate, he might glare.
Head in hands . . . *The incorrigible bad.*
We would act, not so much for any God,
but for Dad.
          Now I spin out of the dark.
The threshing tree's a team of horses
to which I wield feeble, complex reins.
I am the mouthpiece in the circuitry.
My brothers act without question, help
the world where they're able, while I gaze
from this silver bauble like an air-bubble
in a darkened tank, its beauty more and more
false as reports fly up . . .
I cross the bridge to another window,
the big empty barrenness of space.
I admit, *father, father,* through the perspex.

I cannot shake this opposing view of myself,
the responding sight of this tin-machine,
lit and glowing like a hearth, humming
to within microdegrees of efficiency.
My face – blond and blue-eyed – visible
in the port, as if I've been served up
for some act, some omission. I don't know.

The valley history

Over wind-eroded, bleached badlands,
creaking packs come past buttress and crevasse

through which scrolls of Chinese silk unfold,
beside green glassware from Alexandria,

poised bronze wrought in the dust of Rome
and Indian lattice-work, ivory figurines.

With an almost audible sigh of the road,
merchants and drovers lower themselves

to the lush place, benignant Bamiyan's
sweet water, bird-song, best of all its shade.

Their hearts livened by its fine excess.
The valley gives rest beside standing pools.

There is time and reason enough to praise.
A million hammer blows hollow a place

for rough giants daubed with mud and straw,
for feet and face and Buddhas' folded robes

in plaster-work, paint – one red, one blue –
their moonlike features, loose, gilded hands.

Yellow-robed priests are like tiny flowers
that spring beneath each benevolent gaze

by day and night, a new thousand years.
In brief intervals between battles that ebb

and flow indifferently now,
Kalashnikovs stashed between the toes

of the red figure – dry there, defendable.
Smooth head and sloping shoulder of the blue

irrupt orange as an order of dust rolls down
and the cry is *All we are breaking is stone.*

Charismatic

His first works were no more than questions.
Quickly, he put such playthings aside

as the boy became a man with a poet's
booming voice. He was not lost for words,

a maker, whose life, like his fierce Muse,
reviled vagueness. Mama would have seized

self-sacrifice for him had the moment arisen.
But now whole villages make up part

of the poem he is engaged on. Clean as a whistle,
he may be seen at home, plucking the lyre

of his country, while long, rabblous lines
(untidy, impossible to be part of the plan)

clutter roads, suffer unacknowledged losses.
In the camps, there are no civilians listed.

There are no snipers who might be referred to.
He discusses what's what, washes you clean.

He is a puritan who allows the rape
of women in his work. A revolutionary

who knows power is best kept in his hands.
A prophet re-drafting the future

to his own design. An artist whose clear self-
portrait clouds the face of his country.

A man who believes in mother and home,
knows love is the reason many more may die.

The brief occasion of Bosko and Admira

Near the Vrbana Bridge,
on Miljacka River,
in an embrace that none
will tear apart, two lovers together.

I am witness to this
and have been so before,
dispassionate, I see
a clinch that too late lent no protection

on Wednesday at four,
though Bosko, Admira,
had secured permission
to cross the lines that ran through their city.

From sides of the divide,
they were childhood sweethearts.
Lovers then, they flowered
in the free air of Sarajevo, where

they studied chemistry,
each other's fidgeting
on the lab's wooden stools.
Bosko, Admira warmed to each other

in love's dissolution,
they dashed through seven
courtly and careful years
till they had saved some money, found a flat

to which they'll not return.
And both knew their witness:
ubiquitous and cool,
I run from the swan-necked taps in the lab

down to Vrbana Bridge,
the Miljacka River.
I'm the vigour in grass
that's crushed where Bosko and Admira lie.

I'm the little moisture
that remains in their eyes.
The root of erosion.
I am infinitely malleable

long-memoried and clear.
I'm intimate with all,
will eddy, alter shape.
I teem and drive and slake and drown and now

Bosko and Admira,
these two, a recent find,
lie half on the pavement
and half on the lawn where they used to walk.

There, facedown, Bosko sprawls,
his right arm awkwardly
bent on his back; his girl's
left arm wrapped as a belt about his waist

just as they used to do,
lying out in the sun,
with the other lovers
and so few saw any reason for fear.

This is easy for me
as I speak unconfined . . .
On Wednesday at four,
they had permission from the warring sides

for this, their lovers' dash
along the grassy bank
of Miljacka River,
both clutching at bags but utterly exposed –

                    simultaneously
              flung down as they get hit.
              Instantly, Bosko falls
       but Admira has moments left to live.

              She spends them all crawling
                 to where her lover lies
              and hugs him round the waist.
     They die like that, each in the other's arms

              and the river reflects
                 it as a simple truth –
              maybe gilds a little –
        though as rivers always do, I run on.

              The tears of Admira
              slowly dry. The blood spilt
              dries too and a warm breeze
         begins the slick work of desiccation

              in which I find myself
              new form and shape and place,
                 vaporous for a while.
        I gaze down in the old buffeting wind

              and think that if I lived
              as you, I'd watch the clouds,
                 listen to the river,
        walk out and take a lesson from the rain

              that whispers *strike your chains*
                 till perspective's a word
                 you cannot comprehend
            like Bosko, Admira, wanting to break

                 the confine of themselves –
                 suck out the bitterness
                 of their brief occasion
        and love like them and you will be like me.

On night's estate

The longer I stare, the blacked-out
expanses grow more hard to look into –
unlike the United States, unsheathing
its gleaming Floridan sword,
its rash of yellow citidots.
The earth is on fire
south of the Great Lakes' blue pools,
grows more black, but not empty,
out through standing
mid-west corn, block on starry block,
swept to the Pacific's violet edge.

There, shy Australia lies on display.
A single lemon necklace,
loose from Brisbane to Adelaide.
The monumental Asiatic blacks,
their spilt drops of gold
spattering Europe, where it grows
lighter from east to west.
The cobra-squirm of the Nile
is a slithering focus to a blazing delta.

We are those who show ourselves
most clearly when we sleep.
We become like children,
sprawled, unconscious and equal
to the next lamplight.
The world in numerable parts.
Our dreams, a ferocious inequality,
as no-one lives in the Icelandic
inky black, the soot-back of Canada,
the Arctic, ebony of Antarctica,
the emptied Amazon basin,
the Russian steppes, Himalayan pitch.

Whatever life goes on there,
it keeps such a quiet light.
A few red sores of flaming oil-fields.
The indigo of burning forest
in the bulb of Brazil.
And across central Africa,
fat Africa is the body of dark
I hear cry out the kind of catastrophe
it will take to revive the night's wrap.
Let darkness fall as it now appears:
beneath the close of twelve billion lids,
the monster is asleep and dreams of stars.